Blue

David Zwirner Books

ekphrasis

Blue
Derek Jarman

on days like this as a child I
walled myself indoors with my chemistry
set or cut paper fishes to swim in
the bath. Pasted up my stamp collection
and pressed my face against the glass
watching the rain splash over the
gutters and the tailspray of the
sad black cars of the 1950s passing
with their headlights on — Ten
years later I sat and wrote
desultory poems

              the days are numbered
              our love framed & glazed
              reflects shadows
              diverts the mind
              erases harboured thoughts
              erases anchored days
              waiting

and now the dandelion clock has
                        stopped

That seems so like my state of
mind today. Thirty years later
Nicholas of Cusa is most
timely when he says —
The concept of a clock enfolds all
succession in Time. In the concept
the sixth hour is not earlier than

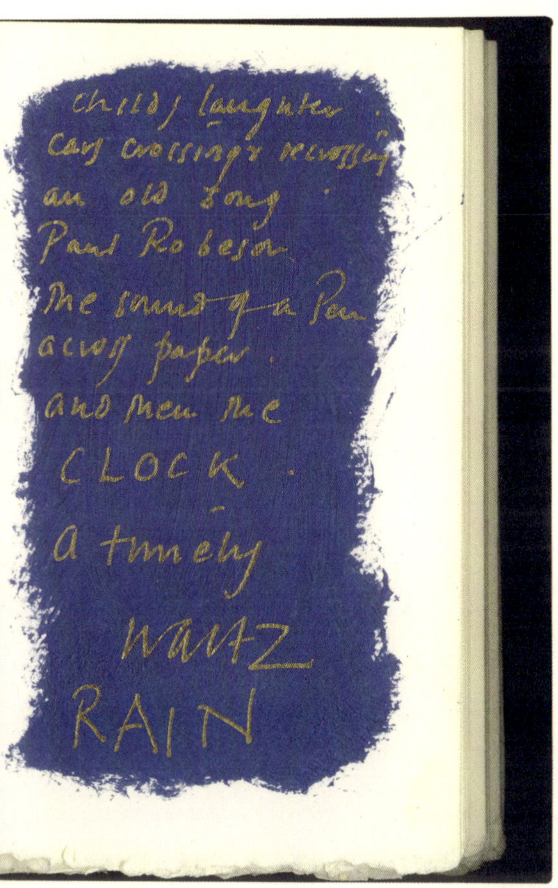

Spread from Derek Jarman, *A Blueprint for Bliss*, 1989

Contents

Introduction

Michael Charlesworth

There is one image in this film: the color blue, filling the screen, with no design, no picture, no inscription, no superimposition to vary the image. And there is a soundtrack. The combination induces a mixture of reflections. The British artist Derek Jarman made *Blue* (1993), his last and best-known film, at the end of his life. Although he was severely physically and visually impaired by 1993, and died of an AIDS-related illness early in the following year, it would be a mistake to assume that he made the film as a single color without sets, actors, story, and the rest of the usual paraphernalia of feature-film making simply because he was debilitated and lacked the energy to organize all the above. In fact, he had been thinking about whether to make the film without images since at least 1987, when he had plenty of energy and strength.[1] The film was therefore the result of an aesthetic decision. "This is the first feature," Jarman announced, "to embrace the intellectual imperative of abstraction."[2] In these words, he declared a center of interest in abstraction and therefore in the art of painting. He continued in a cheerfully grandiose way: "It takes film to the boundary of the known world." *Blue* is also a rare film in that it was broadcast over the radio. At the precise time it was shown on television,[3] the BBC's Radio 3 broadcast the soundtrack, and alert listeners may have availed themselves of the opportunity, offered in advance, to send away for a blue postcard to contemplate over while listening.[4]

The image track is therefore truly abstract, the color having been generated in a film laboratory as a wavelength of light and captured for the seventy-nine minutes of the finished feature on 35 mm film stock.[5] Yet the abstraction of the work is not absolute, in the sense that the dense soundtrack is strongly concrete, featuring music, noises, whispers, voices speaking poetry or conversational-sounding prose, singing and chanting, footsteps on a beach, mechanical sounds of a bicycle rushing past, a washing machine whirring, and a refrigerator defrosting, and, at the beginning, intermittently during the film, and at the end, ringing Tibetan bells. Such bells were used in Tibetan Buddhism to call forth deities or celestial beings and to dismiss them at the end of a ritual—and to help meditation. Any of these uses would have appealed to Jarman, who was interested in inducing reverie and mental drift in audiences,[6] and who would have wanted whatever deities that may exist to witness the predicament of a man in an advanced stage of an AIDS-related illness, which is the subject of *Blue*. To be precise, the subject matter consists of a lament for a generation cut down by HIV/AIDS, and of the difficulties and thoughts, informed by a range of feelings, together with auditory impressions, of a man confronting his own treatment and mortality (the man being Jarman himself, of course). So we can think of *Blue* in terms of abstraction, but not as an entirely nonfigurative work of art, as the soundtrack conveys figuration (or its audible equivalent).

Jarman was a student at the Slade School of Fine Art, at University College London, which he left in 1967 with

Still from *Blue* (1993)

a specialization in theater design and a marked taste for abstraction, which he immediately employed in his design for the Royal Ballet's production *Jazz Calendar* (1968) and exhibitions of his paintings and sculptures at Lisson Gallery (1969). In both cases, the abstraction wasn't absolute. Elongated iron panels, filled with green chips of stone, that stretched across the floor of Lisson Gallery were called *Long Graves* (1969), acknowledging a connection, perhaps a source, in conventional cemetery furniture. In *Jazz Calendar*, the sets were abstract but the dancers brought an inevitable element of figuration (and we might note that the scene titled "Wednesday" was lit entirely by blue light).

In addition to abstraction, the image track of *Blue* rather obviously features monochrome. Jarman had a long-standing interest in the powers of monochrome, dating back to his seminal student days at the Slade. His model proposal for a set design for Jean-Paul Sartre's play *No Exit* shows a crimson stage on which three chairs are placed: one green, one black, and one blue.[7] Such a use of a monochrome background that allows other colors to stand out persists in Jarman's landscape paintings of the 1960s and '70s. In 1981, he made a black painting, *The Spirit of the World*.[8] The gray inscription on it, in Jarman's handwriting, reads: "Caught in the web of Capital." Two paintings from 1983 show a complete use of monochrome: *Untitled (Yellow Painting - The Pleasures of Italy)* and *Untitled (Yellow Painting - Archeologies)* (p. 13).[9] The former is inscribed with the words "lux, calme" and "The

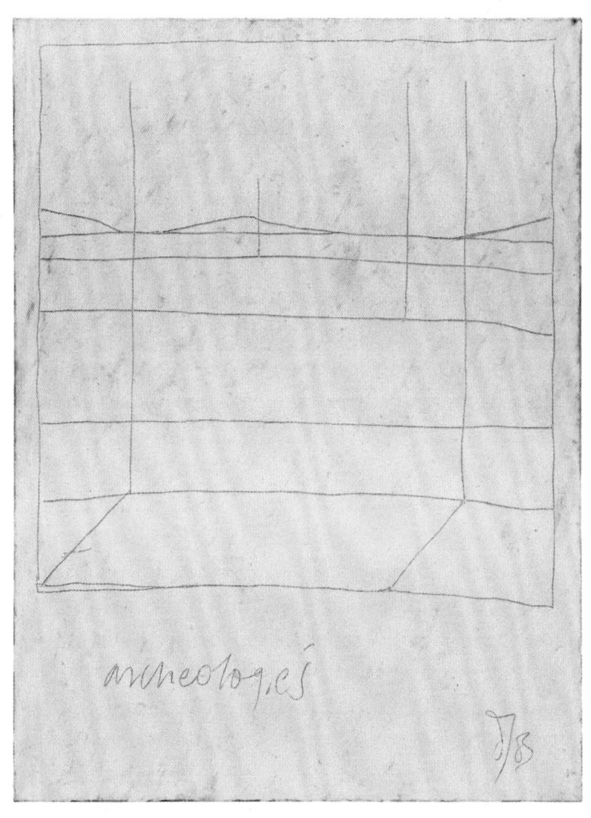

Derek Jarman, *Untitled (Yellow Painting - Archeologies)*, 1983. Oil on canvas,
53 × 40 inches | 134.6 × 101.6 cm

pleasures of Italy," and the latter, "archeologies." In each, warm yellow paint laps up to the edges of the canvas, and marks scored across recall landscape drawings. We can appreciate in these monochromatic examples that their complete effect and significance depend on the combination of visual and verbal elements. (The black painting, *The Spirit of the World*, is subtly reflective, dimly showing the viewer's face above the inscription; the implication is telling enough.) It seems that Jarman, who earned a degree in literature and history at King's College London before undertaking his fine-art courses at the Slade, found a way of working that could answer the demands of his temperament. The combination of word and image recurs in his paintings, with a few exceptions, such as his *GBH* series (1983–1984), but complete monochrome rarely appears again until a small black painting of 1986, *Dead Souls Whisper*, and then the film *Blue*.

Many of Jarman's paintings from the 1980s are small and feature the color black, in the form of paint or even tar, and are varied by touches of gold, red, white, and, less frequently, green and blue. In these, the artist has pressed objects into the thickly painted surfaces. In his penultimate feature film, *Wittgenstein* (1993), we can also see the use of black as a background against which other colors stand out. There was a good practical reason for this, as the film was shot in a small studio in Waterloo, including the scene of the philosopher Ludwig Wittgenstein, the economist John Maynard Keynes, and the dancer Lydia Lopokova playing the planets game (see

p. 16).[10] Nevertheless, the decision wasn't merely practical. "Black velvet registers as infinity on film with no form or boundary," Jarman wrote, "a black without end, that lurks behind the blue sky."[11] *Wittgenstein* shows characters interacting and introduces the audience to elements in Wittgenstein's philosophy, in addition to his sexuality, in a setting of the infinite as a way for the filmmaker to pull a sense of the eternal and its contrast—the transient—into relationship.

In *Blue* there is also a version of infinity. One of the poems in the soundtrack states that the color blue is "An infinite possibility / Becoming tangible."[12] This paradoxical meeting of opposites stems from the thoughts of the French artist Yves Klein. Jarman's first idea for the film, from 1987, which he developed in a notebook dated 1989 and titled *A Blueprint for Bliss* (see pp. 4–5), was to dedicate the film to Klein and to include in the soundtrack a conversation between Jarman and Saint Rita of Cascia, the patron saint of lost causes.[13] Eventually, this idea of celebrating Klein gave way to the subject of AIDS, though a last vestige of it occurs in *Blue* in the paragraph of the voice-over invoking Saint Rita. Jarman went beyond the initial influence, propelled toward creating a different and more encompassing work. Jarman used notebooks (though usually bigger and not as beautiful as *Bliss*) rather than storyboards, treatments, and scripts as a way to work out ideas for his films. He famously disliked narrative and tried to shun it as an approach to filmmaking. The notebooks ensured that scenes and individual shots

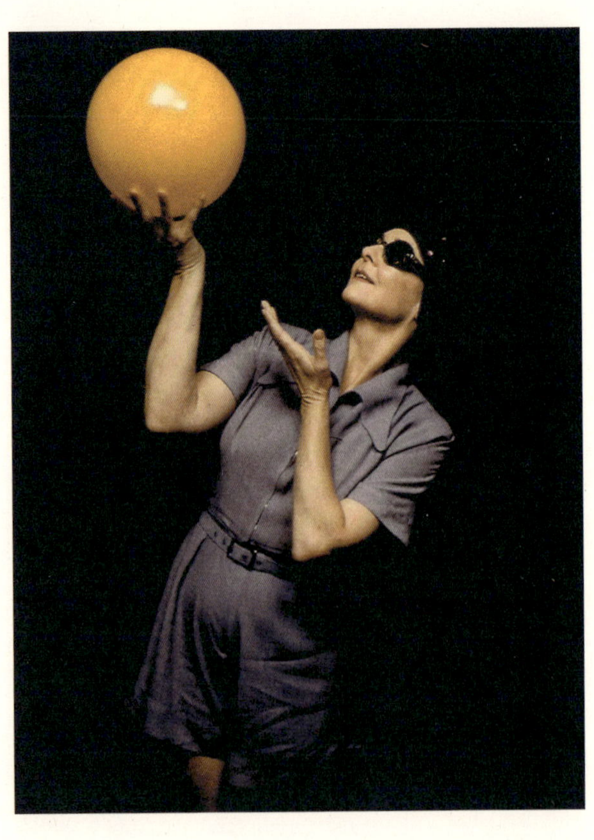

Still from *Wittgenstein* (1993), directed by Derek Jarman

were paramount from the beginning. Concepts for individual shots could be developed or rejected as the pages of the notebook unfolded and the ideas went through several iterations. His notebooks helped him to avoid or downplay the process whereby films, an essentially visual medium, are developed and sold on the basis of words read silently (in the form of treatments and scripts). Jarman found this to be an inhibiting contradiction.

The separation of the soundtrack from the image track in *Blue* elevates another tendency prepared for earlier in other artists' film work. There was, of course, a lively cinema genre that had already made this separation, including work by some of Jarman's favorite filmmakers, such as Kenneth Anger, Jean Genet, and Sergei Parajanov. Within Jarman's oeuvre, his first feature film, *Sebastiane* (1976), takes the preliminary step toward the genre, to the extent that the dialogue is in Latin, with the English translation provided in subtitles and therefore read (silently) by the audience. The actors provide expression through tone of voice; in a word, feeling. But it is Jarman's Super 8 works from 1972 to 1985 that more fully separate image and sound. Through them, he developed his expertise and judgment in stitching the two elements together, though not into the mimetic, naturalistic relationship common in the commercial feature-film industry.[14]

As James Mackay, the film producer who facilitated *Blue*'s making, emphasizes, the subject of the film is a dying man looking out at the world, which was a welcome perspective, as most other attempts to depict the experience of AIDS showed stricken men prematurely aged, emaciated, unable to balance. In other words, attempts to show the extremity of the condition ended up making an unhelpful spectacle of it.[15] Jarman's film avoids this. It is noteworthy that despite the crisis it conjures, the film never breaks down into sobbing, screams, moans, or incoherence. Jarman maintains aesthetic control and poise to the end. Control is maintained even in the paragraphs that describe despair.

His enraged, barely coherent, vengeful feelings instead found expression in painting, in particular in the *Queer* (1992) and *Evil Queen* (1993) series. These big paintings deface and attack the hostility directed toward gay and queer lives in the press at the time. In one work of the *Queer* series, the artist scrawled over photocopies of a hateful page from the gutter press, "SODOMY STRAIGHT / HERE'S NEWS FOR YOU / 40% OF BRITISH WOMEN / TAKE IT UP THE ARSE / YOU CALLED IT MURDER / BUT I CALLED IT LOVE / SPREAD THE PLAGUE." For some people, this might be shocking. Could he really have been advocating for the spread of HIV/AIDS through deliberate infection?[16] Jarman wrote in his diary, "One day the paintings will be seen as more than tantrums and will be seen to be wet with my tears."[17]

The abstract multicolored *Evil Queen* paintings combine paint flung, or clawed, onto the canvas in seemingly feverish gestures with deeply ironic inscriptions scored across them. "Ataxia AIDS is fun" and "Dizzy Bitch" call attention to symptoms of the illness. And there are inscriptions imbued with bitter frustration: "Fuck Me Blind"; "Scream"; "Dead Sexy"; "Blind Fate Let's Fuck"; "Death." The results can be appalling. While beautiful, the paintings can induce a feeling of horror. By contrast, in *Blue* Jarman manages to hold on to his stoicism, and its subject inspires the extraordinarily beautiful poetry of the final section of the film. In *Blue*, aesthetic poise and control have been achieved and by virtue of a different medium having allowed, even demanded, a radically contrasting response.

Within *Blue*, there are even some jeux d'esprit. Various scholars have debated over the pronouns used in the film, asking whom the word "you" refers to. And one must therefore extend this question, by linguistic implication, to wondering who the "I" is as well.[18] This is a false dilemma. One of the most notable of the jeux d'esprit seems to be an Italo Calvino–like allegory of the artist's present state: an account of blinding, induced by external factors, on a journey to the city of Aqua Vitae and the discovery of the "archaeology of sound." Jarman had already used archaeology as a metaphor in his work multiple times: in painting, such as *Untitled (Yellow Painting - Archeologies)*; in his written memoirs; and in his form of cinema, which he characterized as an "archaeology of soul."[19] Thus the "archaeology of sound" provides a wonderful metaphor that conveys the feeling of strangeness Jarman felt in making the film, yet also asserts a continuity with his major interests: painting, writing, and film. As it is the personification of "Blue," a blinded character in the film, we realize something about Blue (who is woken up at the beginning of the film and whose grave is decorated with a *pothos* flower at the end)—he is less a different figure, a "character" in the film, than an alter ego of Jarman himself.

Blue has become an internationally acclaimed work, with many people regarding it as Jarman's greatest film. It won awards and brought him standing ovations at film festivals. The film's stature as a monument to the approximately forty million people who have died of AIDS-related illnesses has only grown, and its importance has deepened in the years since it was made. To make *Blue*, to talk straightforwardly and unflinchingly about his illness and its effects, on his behalf and that of other people living with HIV/AIDS, to make a poet and filmmaker's beautiful work of art out of the extremity of his predicament, was Jarman's affirmation.

1   Michael Charlesworth, *Derek Jarman* (London: Reaktion Books, 2011), p. 174.

2   Derek Jarman, *Smiling in Slow Motion*, ed. Keith Collins (London: Century, 2000), p. 320.

3   By Britain's Channel 4 in September 1993.

4   Tony Peake, *Derek Jarman: A Biography* (1999; New York: The Overlook Press, 2000), p. 527. Peake's quietly magisterial book is the definitive biography of Jarman.

5   Information from James Mackay, the film's producer. The film's transfer to digital medium has allowed for the color to be readjusted to appear closer to International Klein Blue, one of Jarman's early ideas for the work.

6   Francesca Balboni describes one aspect of this, based on Jarman's use of "camera reality," in her article "Burning Through: Derek Jarman's Realism in *The Last of England* (1987)," *Oxford Art Journal* (August 2019): pp. 217–231.

7   A fireplace and doorway are called forward from the background array by flakes of gold around them, showing through the crimson paint.

8   Email to the author from Amanda Wilkinson, June 23, 2020.

9   These two paintings were shown at Amanda Wilkinson Gallery, London, in 2021, and are illustrated in the related publication *Derek Jarman: When yellow wishes to ingratiate it becomes gold* (London: Brewer Street Press, 2021).

10   Peake, *Derek Jarman*, p. 508.

11   Derek Jarman, *Chroma* (1994; New York: The Overlook Press, 1995), p. 137.

12   This volume, p. 33.

13   The image on pp. 4–5 reproduces a double-page spread from this notebook. Like all the right-hand pages in the book, the page painted blue is inscribed in gold ink with indications for sound effects. We can assume the texts on the left-hand pages are drafts for voiceovers.

14   See James Mackay, *Derek Jarman Super 8* (London: Thames and Hudson; Zurich: Luma Foundation, 2014), and Jarman's films *Imagining October* (1984), *The Angelic Conversation* (1985), and *The Last of England* (1987), together with the later (and only partially shot in Super 8) *War Requiem* (1989).

15   Conversation with the author, October 2021. On this, see Jim Ellis's excellent account of *Blue*, in Jim Ellis, *Derek Jarman's Angelic Conversation* (Minneapolis: University of Minnesota Press, 2009), pp. 242–245, quoting Douglas Crimp.

16   "These are tactless pictures," wrote Simon Watney, "which draw attention to ugly emotions in order to refute them." From his essay "Rewriting History," in *Derek Jarman: Queer*. Exh. cat. (Manchester, England: Manchester City Art Galleries and Richard Salmon Ltd, 1992), n.p.

17   Jarman, *Smiling in Slow Motion*, p. 303.

18   They include Rowland Wymer, *Derek Jarman* (Manchester, England: Manchester University Press, 2005); Ellis, *Derek Jarman's Angelic Conversation*; Steven Dillon, *Derek Jarman and Lyric Film: The Mirror and the Sea* (Austin: University of Texas Press, 2004).

19   Derek Jarman, *Kicking the Pricks* (London: Vintage, 1996), p. 235. *Kicking the Pricks* is the second edition of a book originally published by Constable in 1987 under the title *The Last of England*.

Blue: Text of the Film by Derek Jarman

You say to the boy open your eyes

When he opens his eyes and sees the light

You make him cry out. Saying

O Blue come forth

O Blue arise

O Blue ascend

O Blue come in

I am sitting with some friends in this café drinking coffee served by young refugees from Bosnia. The war rages across the newspapers and through the ruined streets of Sarajevo.

Tania said "Your clothes are on back to front and inside out." Since there were only two of us here I took them off and put them right then and there. I am always here before the doors open.

What need of so much news from abroad while all that concerns either life or death is all transacting and at work within me.

I step off the kerb and a cyclist nearly knocks me down.
Flying in from the dark he nearly parted my hair.

I step into a blue funk.

The doctor in St Bartholomew's Hospital thought he
could detect lesions in my retina – the pupils dilated
with belladonna – the torch shone into them with a terrible blinding light.

    Look left

    Look down

    Look up

    Look right

    Blue flashes in my eyes.

    Blue Bottle buzzing

    Lazy days

    The sky blue butterfly

    Sways on a cornflower

Lost in the warmth

Of the blue heat haze

Singing the blues

Quiet and slowly

Blue of my heart

Blue of my dreams

Slow blue love

Of delphinium days

Blue is the universal love in which man bathes – it is the
terrestrial paradise.

I'm walking along the beach in a howling gale –

Another year is passing

In the roaring waters

I hear the voices of dead friends

Love is life that lasts forever.

My heart's memory turns to you

David.   Howard.   Graham.   Terry.   Paul . . .

But what if this present

Were the world's last night

In the setting sun your love fades

Dies in the moonlight

Fails to rise

Thrice denied by cock crow

In the dawn's first light

Look down

Look left

Look up

Look right

The camera flash

Atomic bright

Photos

The CMV – a green moon then the world turns
magenta

My retina

Is a distant planet

A red Mars

From a *Boy's Own* comic

With yellow infection

Bubbling at the corner

I said this looks like a planet

The doctor says – "Oh, I think

It looks like a pizza"

The worst of the illness is the uncertainty. I've played
this scenario back and forth each hour of the day for
the last six years.

Blue transcends the solemn geography of human limits.

   I am home with the blinds drawn

   H.B. is back from Newcastle

   But gone out – the washing

   Machine is roaring away

   And the fridge is defrosting

   These are his favourite sounds

I've been given the option of being an in-patient at the hospital or coming in twice a day to be hooked to a drip. My vision will never come back.

The retina is destroyed, though when the bleeding stops what is left of my sight might improve. I have to come to terms with sightlessness.

If I lose half my sight will my vision be halved?

The virus rages fierce. I have no friends now who are not dead or dying. Like a blue frost it caught them. At work, at the cinema, on marches and beaches. In churches on their knees, running, flying, silent or shouting protest.

It started with sweats in the night and swollen glands. Then the black cancers spread across their faces – as they fought for breath TB and pneumonia hammered at the lungs, and Toxo at the brain. Reflexes scrambled – sweat poured through hair matted like lianas in the tropical forest. Voices slurred – and then were lost forever. My pen chased this story across the page tossed this way and that in the storm.

The blood of sensibility is blue

I consecrate myself

To find its most perfect expression

My sight failed a little more in the night

H.B. offers me his blood

It will kill everything he says

The drip of DHPG

Trills like a canary

I am accompanied by a shadow into which H.B. appears and disappears. I have lost the sight on the periphery of my right eye.

I hold out my hands before me and slowly part them. At a certain moment they disappear out of the corner of my eyes. This is how I used to see. Now if I repeat the motion, this is all I see.

I shall not win the battle against the virus – in spite of the slogans like 'Living with AIDS'. The virus was appropriated by the well – so we have to live with AIDS while they spread the quilt for the moths of Ithaca across the wine dark sea.

Awareness is heightened by this, but something else is lost. A sense of reality drowned in theatre.

Thinking blind, becoming blind.

In the hospital it is as quiet as a tomb. The nurse fights to find a vein in my right arm. We give up after five attempts. Would you faint if someone stuck a needle into your arm? I've got used to it – but I still shut my eyes.

The Gautama Buddha instructs me to walk away from illness.

But he wasn't attached to a drip.

Fate is the strongest

Fate Fated Fatal

I resign myself to Fate

Blind Fate

The drip stings

A lump swells up in my arm

Out comes the drip

An electric shock sparks up my arm

How can I walk away with a drip attached to me?

How am I going to walk away from this?

I fill this room with the echo of many voices

Who passed time here

Voices unlocked from the blue of the long dried paint

The sun comes and floods this empty room

I call it my room

My room has welcomed many summers

Embraced laughter and tears

Can it fill itself with your laughter

Each word a sunbeam

Glancing in the light

This is the song of My Room

David.   Howard.   Graham.   Terry.   Paul.

Blue stretches, yawns and is awake.

There is a photo in the newspaper this morning of refugees leaving Bosnia. They look out of time. Peasant
women with scarves and black dresses stepped from
the pages of an older Europe. One of them has lost her
three children.

Lightning flickers through the hospital window – at the
door an elderly woman stands waiting for the rain to

clear. I ask her if I can give her a lift, I've hailed a taxi. "Can you take me to Holborn tube?" On the way she breaks down in tears. She has come from Edinburgh. Her son is in the ward – he has meningitis and has lost the use of his legs – I'm helpless as the tears flow. I can't see her. Just the sound of her sobbing.

One can know the whole world

Without stirring abroad

Without looking out of the window

One can see the way of heaven

The further one goes

The less one knows

In the pandemonium of image

I present you with the universal Blue

Blue an open door to soul

An infinite possibility
Becoming tangible

Here I am again in the waiting room. Hell on Earth is
a waiting room. Here you know you are not in control
of yourself, waiting for your name to be called: "712213".
Here you have no name, confidentiality is nameless.
Where is 666? Am I sitting opposite him/her? Maybe
666 is the demented woman switching the channels on
the TV.

What do I see

Past the gates of conscience

Activists invading Sunday Mass

In the cathedral

An epic Czar Ivan denouncing the

Patriarch of Moscow

A moon-faced boy who spits and repeatedly

Crosses himself – as he genuflects

Will the pearly gates slam shut in

The faces of the devout

The demented woman is discussing needles – there is always a discussion of needles here. She has a line put into her neck.

How are we perceived, if we are to be perceived at all? For the most part we are invisible.

If the doors of Perception were cleansed then everything would be seen as it is.

The dog barks, the caravan passes.
Marco Polo stumbles across the Blue Mountain.

Marco Polo stops and sits on a lapis throne by the River Oxus while he is ministered to by the descendants of Alexander the Great. The caravan approaches, blue canvasses fluttering in the wind. Blue people from over the sea – ultramarine – have come to collect the lapis with its flecks of gold.

The road to the city of Aqua Vitae is protected by a labyrinth built from crystals and mirrors which in the sunlight cause terrible blindness. The mirrors reflect each of your betrayals, magnify them and drive you into madness.

Blue walks into the labyrinth. Absolute silence is demanded of all its visitors, so their presence does not disturb the poets who are directing the excavations. Digging can only proceed on the calmest of days as rain and wind destroy the finds.

The archaeology of sound has only just been perfected and the systematic cataloguing of words has until recently been undertaken in a haphazard way. Blue watched as a word or phrase materialised in scintillating sparks, a poetry of fire which cast everything into darkness with the brightness of its reflections.

As a teenager I used to work for the Royal National Institute for the Blind on their Christmas appeal for radios, with dear Miss Punch, seventy years old, who used to arrive each morning on her Harley Davidson.

She kept us on our toes. Her job as a gardener gave her time to spare in January. Miss Punch Leather Woman was the first out dyke I ever met. Closeted and frightened by my sexuality she was my hope. "Climb on, let's go for a ride." She looked like Edith Piaf, a sparrow, and wore a cock-eyed beret at a saucy angle. She bossed all the other old girls who came back year after year for her company.

In the paper today. Three quarters of the AIDS organisations are not providing safer sex information. One district said they had no queers in their community, but you might try district X – they have a theatre.

TB or not TB, that is the question.

My sight seems to have closed in. The hospital is even quieter this morning. Hushed. I have a sinking feeling in my stomach. I feel defeated. My mind bright as a button but my body falling apart – a naked light bulb in a dark and ruined room. There is death in the air here but we're not talking about it. But I know the silence might be broken by distraught visitors screaming, "Help Sister! Help Nurse!" followed by the sound of feet rushing along the corridor. Then silence.

Blue protects white from innocence

Blue drags black with it

Blue is darkness made visible

Blue protects white from innocence

Blue drags black with it

Blue is darkness made visible

Over the mountains is the shrine to Rita, where all at the end of the line call. Rita is the Saint of the Lost Cause. The saint of all who are at their wit's end, who are hedged in and trapped by the facts of the world. These facts, detached from cause, trapped the Blue Eyed Boy in a system of unreality. Would all these blurred facts that deceive dissolve in his last breath? For accustomed to believing in image, an absolute idea of value, his world had forgotten the command of essence: Thou Shall Not Create Unto Thyself Any Graven Image, although you know the task is to fill the empty page. From the bottom of your heart, pray to be released from image.

The image is a prison of the soul, your heredity, your education, your vices and aspirations, your qualities, your psychological world.

I have walked behind the sky.

For what are you seeking?

The fathomless blue of Bliss.

To be an astronaut of the void, leave the comfortable house that imprisons you with reassurance.
Remember,

To be going and to have are not eternal – fight the fear that engenders the beginning, the middle and the end.

For Blue there are no boundaries or solutions.

Time is what keeps the light from reaching us.

How did my friends cross the cobalt river, with what did they pay the ferryman? As they set out for the indigo shore under this jet-black sky – some died on their feet with a backward glance. Did they see Death with the hell hounds pulling a dark chariot, bruised blue-black, growing dark in the absence of light, did they hear the blast of trumpets?

David ran home panicked on the train from Waterloo, brought back exhausted and unconscious to die that night. Terry who mumbled incoherently into his incontinent tears. Others faded like flowers cut by the scythe of the Blue Bearded Reaper, parched as the waters of life receded. Howard turned slowly to stone, petrified day by day, his mind imprisoned in a concrete fortress until all we could hear were his groans on the telephone circling the globe.

Mad Vincent sits on his yellow chair clasping his knees to his chest – Bananas. The sunflowers wilt in the empty pot, bone dry, skeletal, the black seeds picked into the staring face of a halloween pumpkin. He is unaware of Blue standing in the corner. Fevered eyes glare at the jaundiced corn, caw of the jet-black crows spiralling in the yellow. The lemon goblin stares from the unwanted canvasses thrown in a corner. Sourpuss suicide screams with evil – clasping cowardly Yellowbelly, slit-eyed.

Blue fights diseased Yellowbelly whose fetid breath scorches the trees yellow with ague. Betrayal is the oxygen of his devilry. He'll stab you in the back. Yellowbelly places a jaundiced kiss in the air, the stink of pus blinds Blue's eyes. Evil swims in the yellow bile. Yellowbelly's snake eyes poison. He crawls over Eve's rotting apple wasp-like. Quick as a flash he stings Blue in the mouth – "AAAUGH!" – his hellish legions buzz and chuckle in the mustard gas. They'll piss all over you. Sharp nicotine-stained fangs bared. Blue transformed into an insectocutor, his Blue aura frying the foes.

We all contemplated suicide

We hoped for euthanasia

We were lulled into believing

Morphine dispelled pain

Rather than making it tangible

Like a mad Disney cartoon

Transforming itself into

Every conceivable nightmare

Karl killed himself – how did he do it? I never asked. It seemed incidental. What did it matter if he swigged prussic acid or shot himself in the eye. Maybe he dived into the streets from high up in the cloud-lapped skyscrapers.

The nurse explains the implant. You mix the drugs and drip yourself once a day. The drugs are kept in a small fridge they give you.

Can you imagine travelling around with that? The metal implant will set the bomb detector off in airports, and I can just see myself travelling to Berlin with a fridge under my arm.

Impatient youths of the sun

Burning with many colours

Flick combs through hair

In bathroom mirrors

Fucking with fusion and fashion

Dance in the beams of emerald lasers

Mating on suburban duvets

Cum splattered nuclear breeders

What a time that was

The drip ticks out the seconds, the source of a stream along which the minutes flow, to join the river of hours, the sea of years and the timeless ocean.

The side-effects of DHPG, the drug for which I have to come into hospital to be dripped twice a day, are: Low white blood cell count, increased risk of infection, low platelet count which may increase the risk of bleeding, low red blood cell count (anaemia), fever, rash, abnormal liver function, chills, swelling of the body (oedema), infections, malaise, irregular heart beat, high blood pressure (hypertension), low blood pressure (hypotension), abnormal thoughts or dreams, loss of balance (ataxia), coma, confusion, dizziness, headache, nervousness, damage to nerves (paraesthesia), psychosis, sleepiness (somnolence), shaking, nausea, vomiting, loss of appetite (anorexia), diarrhoea, bleeding from the stomach or intestine (intestinal haemorrhage), abdominal pain, increased number of one type of white blood cell, low blood sugar, shortness of breath, hair loss (alopecia), itching (pruritus), hives, blood in the urine, abnormal kidney function, increased blood urea, redness (inflammation), pain or irritation (phlebitis).

Retinal detachments have been observed in patients both before and after initiation of therapy. The drug has caused decreased sperm production in animals and may cause infertility in humans, and birth defects in animals. Although there is no information in human studies, it should be considered a potential carcinogen since it causes tumours in animals.

If you are concerned about any of the above side-effects or if you would like any further information, please ask your doctor.

In order to be put on the drug you have to sign a piece of paper stating you understand that all these illnesses are a possibility.

I really can't see what I am to do. I am going to sign it.

The darkness comes in with the tide

The year slips on the calendar

Your kiss flares

A match struck in the night

Flares and dies

My slumber broken

Kiss me again

Kiss me

Kiss me again

And again

Never enough

Greedy lips

Speedwell eyes

Blue skies

A man sits in a wheelchair, his hair awry, munching through a packet of dried biscuits, slow and deliberate as a praying mantis. He speaks enthusiastically but sometimes incoherently of the hospice. He says, "You can't be too careful who you mix with there, there's no way of telling the visitors, patients or staff apart. The staff have nothing to identify them except they are all into leather. The place is like an S&M club." This hospice has been built by charity, the names of the donors displayed for all to see.

Charity has allowed the uncaring to appear to care and is terrible for those dependent on it. It has become big business as the government shirks its responsibilities in these uncaring times. We go along with this, so the rich and powerful who fucked us over once fuck us over again and get it both ways. We have always been mistreated, so if anyone gives us the slightest sympathy we overreact with our thanks.

I am a mannish

Muff diving

Size queen

With bad attitude

An arse licking

Psychofag

Molesting the flies of privacy

Balling lesbian boys

A perverted heterodemon

Crossing purpose with death

I am a cock sucking

Straight acting

Lesbian man

With ball crushing bad manners

Laddish nymphomaniac politics

Spunky sexist desires

Of incestuous inversion and

Incorrect terminology

I am a Not Gay

H.B. is in the kitchen

Greasing his hair

He guards the space

Against me

He calls it his office

At nine we leave for the hospital

H.B. comes back from the eye dept

Where all my notes are muddled

He says

It's like Romania in there

Two light bulbs

Grimly illuminate

The flaking walls

There is a box of dolls

In a corner

Indescribably grimy

The doctor says

Well of course

The kids don't see them

There are no resources

To brighten the place up

My eyes sting from the drops

The infection has halted

The flash leaves

Scarlet after images

Of the blood vessels in my eye

Teeth chattering February

Cold as death

Pushes at the bedsheets

An aching cold

Interminable as marble

My mind

Frosted with drugs ices up

A drift of empty snowflakes

Whiting out memory

A blinkered twister

Circling in spirals

Cross-eyed meddlesome consciousness

Shall I? Will I?

Doodling death watch

Mind how you go

Oral DHPG is consumed by the liver, so they have tweaked a molecule to fool the system. What risk is there? If I had to live forty years blind, I might think twice. Treat my illness like the dodgems: music, bright lights, bumps and throw yourself into life again.

The pills are the most difficult, some taste bitter, others are too large. I'm taking about thirty a day, a walking chemical laboratory. I gag on them as I swallow them and they come up half dissolved in the coughing and spluttering.

My skin sits on me like the shirt of Nessus. My face irritates, as do my back and legs at night. I toss and turn, scratching, unable to sleep. I get up, turn on the light. Stagger to the bathroom. If I become so tired, maybe I'll sleep. Films chase through my mind. Once in a while I dream a dream as magnificent as the Taj Mahal. I cross southern India with a young spirit guide – India the land of my dreaming childhood. The souvenirs in Moselle's peach and grey living room. Granny called Moselle, called 'Girly', called May. An orphan who lost her name, which was Ruben. Jade monkeys, ivory miniatures, mahjongg. The winds and bamboos of China.

All the old taboos of

Blood lines and blood banks

Blue blood and bad blood

Our blood and your blood

I sit here – you sit there

As I slept a jet slammed into a tower block. The jet was
almost empty but two hundred people were fried in their
sleep.

The earth is dying and we do not notice it.

A young man frail as Belsen

Walks slowly down the corridor

His pale green hospital pyjamas

Hanging off him

It's very quiet

Just the distant coughing

My jugsy eye blots out the

Young man who has walked past

My field of vision

This illness knocks you for six

Just as you start to forget it

A bullet in the back of the head

Might be easier

You know, you can take longer than

The second world war to get to the grave

Ages and Aeons quit the room

Exploding into timelessness

No entrances or exits now

No need for obituaries or final judgements

We knew that time would end

After tomorrow at sunrise

We scrubbed the floors

And did the washing up

It would not catch us unawares

The white flashes you are experiencing in your eyes are common when the retina is damaged.

The damaged retina has started to peel away leaving innumerable black floaters, like a flock of starlings swirling around in the twilight.

I am back at St Mary's to have my eyes looked at by the specialist. The place is the same, but there is new staff. How relieved I am not to have the operation this morning to have a tap put in my chest. I must try and cheer up H.B. as he has had a hell of a fortnight. In the waiting room a little grey man over the way is fretting as he has to get to Sussex. He says, "I am going blind, I cannot read any longer." A little later he picks up a newspaper, struggles with it for a moment and throws it back on the table. My stinging eye-drops have stopped me reading, so I write this in a haze of belladonna. The little grey man's face has fallen into tragedy. He looks like Jean Cocteau without the poet's refined arrogance. The room is full of men and women squinting into the dark in different states of illness. Some barely able to walk, distress and anger on every face and then a terrible resignation.

Jean Cocteau takes off his glasses, he looks about him with an undescribable meanness. He has black slip-on shoes, blue socks, grey trousers, a Fairisle sweater and a herringbone jacket. The posters that plaster the walls above him have endless question marks, HIV/AIDS?, AIDS?, HIV? ARE YOU AFFECTED BY HIV/AIDS? AIDS?, ARC?, HIV? This is a hard wait. The shattering bright light of the eye specialist's camera leaves that empty sky blue after-image. Did I really see green the first time? The after-image dissolves in a second. As the photographs progress, colours change to pink and the light turns to orange. The process is a torture, but the result, stable eyesight, worth the price and the twelve pills I have to take a day. Sometimes looking at them I feel nauseous and want to skip them. It must be my association with H.B., lover of the computer and king of the keyboard that brought my luck on the computer which chose my name for this drug trial. I nearly forgot as I left St Mary's I smiled at Jean Cocteau. He gave a sweet smile back.

I caught myself looking at shoes in a shop window. I thought of going in and buying a pair, but stopped myself. The shoes I am wearing at the moment should be sufficient to walk me out of life.

Pearl fishers

In azure seas

Deep waters

Washing the isle of the dead

In coral harbours

Amphora

      Spill

  Gold

Across the still seabed

We lie there

Fanned by the billowing

Sails of forgotten ships

Tossed by the mournful winds

Of the deep

Lost Boys

Sleep forever

In a dear embrace

Salt lips touching

In submarine gardens

Cool marble fingers

Touch an antique smile

Shell sounds

Whisper

Deep love drifting on the tide forever

The smell of him

Dead good looking

In beauty's summer

His blue jeans

Around his ankles

Bliss in my ghostly eye

Kiss me

On the lips

On the eyes

Our name will be forgotten

In time

No one will remember our work

Our life will pass like the traces of a cloud

And be scattered like

Mist that is chased by the

Rays of the sun

For our time is the passing of a shadow

And our lives will run like

Sparks through the stubble

I place a delphinium, Blue, upon your grave.

BLUE

Written and directed by Derek Jarman
Producers: James Mackay and Takashi Asai
Composer: Simon Fisher Turner
Associate Director: David Lewis
Sound Design: Marvin Black
Re-recording Mixer: Paul Hamblin
A Basilisk Communications production

Voices
Nigel Terry
John Quentin
Derek Jarman
Tilda Swinton

Musicians
Jon Balance
Gini Ball
Marvin Black
Peter Christopherson
Markus Dravius
Brian Eno
Tony Hinnigan
Danny Hyde
Jan Latham Koenig
Marden Hill
The King of Luxembourg
Miranda Sex Garden
Momus
Vini Reilly
Kate St John
Simon Fisher Turner
Richard Watson
Hugh Webb

DEREK JARMAN (1942–1994) was an English artist, film-maker, stage designer, diarist, author, and gardener. He was educated at the King's College London and at the Slade School of Art. In 1967, Jarman exhibited his paintings in *Young Contemporaries*, Tate Gallery, London; Lisson Gallery, London; and Fifth Biennale des Jeunes Artistes, Musée d'Art Moderne, Paris. Jarman worked as a set designer on *Jazz Calendar*, The Royal Ballet, London (1968); *Don Giovanni*, ENO, London Coliseum (1968); Ken Russell's feature films *The Devils* (1971) and *Savage Messiah* (1972); and *The Rake's Progress*, Maggio Musicale, Firenze (1982), among other productions. In the early 1970s, Jarman began an extensive series of filmworks made with Super 8 mm, followed by his first full-length feature film, *Sebastiane*, in 1975. He then went on to make ten feature films, including *Jubilee* (1978); *The Angelic Conversation* (1985); *Caravaggio* (1986); *The Garden* (1990); and *Edward II* (1991). His final film, *Blue*, was first shown at the Biennale Arte, Venice, in 1993. Selected solo exhibitions include Sarah Bradley's Gallery, London (1978); Edward Totah Gallery, London (1982); ICA, London (1984); Richard Salmon Ltd., London (1987); Whitworth Art Gallery, Manchester, England (1994); X Initiative: Phase I, New York (2009); and Julia Stoschek, Dusseldorf (2010). *Blue* was featured in the exhibition *More Life*, David Zwirner, New York, in 2021. Jarman wrote several books, including the autobiographical *Dancing Ledge* (1984) and two volumes of memoirs, *Modern Nature* (1991) and *At Your Own Risk* (1992). *Derek Jarman's Garden*, which documents the creation of his extraordinary garden at Dungeness, Kent, England, was published in 1995.

MICHAEL CHARLESWORTH is a professor of art history at the University of Texas at Austin, teaching nineteenth-century European painting and photography. Specializing in interdisciplinary approaches, he has in recent years written the first full-length study of Reginald Farrer, the early twentieth-century plant collector, gardener, writer, watercolor painter, and Buddhist, and a critical life of Derek Jarman, the late twentieth-century film-maker, painter, writer, designer, and gardener. He has published articles on early photography, the picturesque, and eighteenth-century panoramic drawing, as well as scholarly articles on the gardens of Stourhead, Rievaulx Terrace, and Wentworth Castle. His interdisciplinary study *Landscape and Vision in Nineteenth-Century Britain and France* was published in 2008. Over the past two years, Charlesworth has been writing a second book project about Derek Jarman.

THE *EKPHRASIS* SERIES

"Ekphrasis" is traditionally defined as the literary representation of a work of visual art. One of the oldest forms of writing, it originated in ancient Greece, where it referred to the practice and skill of presenting artworks through vivid, highly detailed accounts. Today, "ekphrasis" is more openly interpreted as one art form, whether it be writing, visual art, music, or film, that is used to define and describe another art form, in order to bring to an audience the experiential and visceral impact of the subject.

The *ekphrasis* series from David Zwirner Books is dedicated to publishing rare, out-of-print, and newly commissioned texts as accessible paperback volumes. It is part of David Zwirner Books's ongoing effort to publish new and surprising pieces of writing on visual culture.

OTHER TITLES IN THE *EKPHRASIS* SERIES

On Contemporary Art
César Aira

Something Close to Music
John Ashbery

The Salon of 1846
Charles Baudelaire

Strange Impressions
Romaine Brooks

A Balthus Notebook
Guy Davenport

Ramblings of a Wannabe Painter
Paul Gauguin

Thrust: A Spasmodic Pictorial History of the Codpiece in Art
Michael Glover

Visions and Ecstasies
H.D.

Mad about Painting
Katsushika Hokusai

Kandinsky: Incarnating Beauty
Alexandre Kojève

Pissing Figures 1280–2014
Jean-Claude Lebensztejn

The Psychology of an Art Writer
Vernon Lee

Degas and His Model
Alice Michel

28 Paradises
Patrick Modiano and Dominique Zehrfuss

Summoning Pearl Harbor
Alexander Nemerov

Chardin and Rembrandt
Marcel Proust

Letters to a Young Painter
Rainer Maria Rilke

The Cathedral Is Dying
Auguste Rodin

Giotto and His Works in Padua
John Ruskin

Duchamp's Last Day
Donald Shambroom

Dix Portraits
Gertrude Stein

Photography and Belief
David Levi Strauss

The Critic as Artist
Oscar Wilde

Oh, to Be a Painter!
Virginia Woolf

Two Cities
Cynthia Zarin

Blue
Derek Jarman

Published by
David Zwirner Books
520 West 20th Street, 3rd Floor
New York, New York 10011
+ 1 212 727 2070
davidzwirnerbooks.com

Editor: Elizabeth Gordon
Editorial Coordinator:
Jessica Palinski
Proofreader: Meg Whiteford
Design: Michael Dyer / Remake
Production Manager: Luke Chase
Color separations: VeronaLibri,
Verona
Printing: VeronaLibri, Verona

Typeface: Arnhem
Paper: Holmen Book Cream, 80 gsm

Publication © 2023
David Zwirner Books
First published 2023. Second
printing 2023

Blue © 1993
Basilisk Communications Ltd

Introduction © 2023
Michael Charlesworth

The right of Derek Jarman to be
identified as Author of this book
has been asserted by him.

The text of *Blue* is reproduced from
the Overlook Press edition (1994)
with permission. In certain specific
cases, we have made minor
amendments to the text to match
the final script of the film.

pp. 4–5: © The Keith Collins Will
Trust/Basilisk Communications Ltd
p. 11: © 1993 Basilisk
Communications Ltd
p. 13: Courtesy Amanda Wilkinson
Gallery London and Keith Collins
Will Trust
p. 16: © BFI. Courtesy the BFI
National Archive

Thanks are due to James Mackay,
and to Michael Charlesworth,
David Lewis, Donald Smith, and
Amanda Wilkinson.

All rights reserved. No part of
this book may be reproduced or
transmitted in any form or by any
means, electronic or mechanical,
including photographing,
recording, or information storage
and retrieval, without prior
permission in writing from the
publisher.

ISBN 978-1-64423-088-6

Library of Congress
Control Number: 2022920411

Printed in Italy